IRELAND for KIDS

365 Fun Facts and Trivia for Little Lads and Lasses

CIEL PUBLISHING

© 2023 Ciel Publishing. All rights reserved.

The contents of this book may not be reproduced, duplicated or transmitted without direct written permission from the author.

Legal Notice:
You cannot amend, distribute, sell, use, quote or paraphrase any part of the content of this book without the consent of the author.

Disclaimer Notice:
Please note the information contained in this document is for educational and entertainment purposes only. No warranties of any kind are expressed or implied. Readers acknowledge that the author is not engaging in the rendering of legal, financial, medical or professional advice.

By reading this document, the reader agrees that under no circumstances is the author responsible for any losses, direct or indirect, which are incurred as a result of the use of the information contained within this document, including, but not limited to, errors, omissions, or inaccuracies.

Welcome to Ireland!

IRELAND

Former name	:	Dominus Hiberniae
Official name	:	Republic of Ireland
Capital city	:	Dublin
Language	:	English, Irish
Currency	:	Euro
Total area	:	84,421 km2

NATIONAL SYMBOLS

National Day	:	March 17th
National Anthem	:	Amhran Na BhFiann
National Currency	:	Euro
National Colors	:	Green, White and Orange
National Animal	:	Irish Hare
National Bird	:	Northern Lapwing
National Sweet	:	Irish Barmbrack
National Dish	:	Irish Stew
National Tree	:	Sessile oak
National Flower	:	Shamrock

TABLE OF CONTENTS

9
Introduction

11
Chapter 1
Enchanting Myths and Fables

17
Chapter 2
The Fascinating Facts of Scenic Spots

23
Chapter 3
Delicious Delights and Irish Treats

30
Chapter 4
Victorious Sports and Champion Athletes

33
Chapter 5
Amazing Creatures and Wild Animals

38
Chapter 6
Epic Adventures and Folktales

41
Chapter 7
Celebrated Celebrities and Famous Folks

44
Chapter 8
Educational Excursions and Literary Legends

48
Chapter 9
Melodic Memories and Groovy Rhythms

52
Chapter 10
Bizarre Bits and Unbelievable Truths

56
Chapter 11
Unbelievable Irish History Trivia

61
Chapter 12
Tongue Twisters and Celtic Chuckles

68
Chapter 13
Basic Irish Words

73
Conclusion

78
Thank You!

DID YOU KNOW?

Ireland is an island off the coast of Europe. Most of it is a country named the Republic of Ireland. Moreover, the island has a region known as Northern Ireland, which is actually part of the United Kingdom, a country that is also made up of England, Scotland, and Wales. Whereas the United Kingdom is ruled by a king or queen, the Republic of Ireland has a President, much like the United States. However, like the UK, Ireland's second-in-command is the Prime Minister—well, the Taoiseach, which means Prime Minister in the Irish language.

INTRODUCTION

Céad mile fáilte!

Hiya, weans! Welcome to our book of fascinating facts about the amazing place that is Ireland.

If you're reading this anywhere that isn't Ireland, you may think that you already know a lot about the place: green clothes, fun dances, red hair, shamrocks, and Guinness beer. Maybe you recognize the typical Irish accent, especially if you've heard it being used by one of the many international Irish celebrities, like Liam Neeson, Saoirse Ronan, or Bono. But we're here to tell you that there is so much more to learn about this tiny island.

You're in luck, because there is a whole world of fascinating things to learn about Ireland. Saint Patrick wasn't actually Irish, and he didn't truly banish all the snakes from Ireland. Most Irish people are brunettes, not redheads, and most of them don't drink Guinness—there are better brands of beer out there, after all. Stick with us and discover the fascinating world of the Emerald Isle.

DID YOU KNOW?

What is the Irish language, you ask? It's a language spoken by Irish people for thousands of years, also called Gaelic. When Ireland became a part of the British Empire, they were forced to start speaking English as well. Today, everyone in Ireland speaks English, with their own distinct accent. Only around 39% of Irish people can speak Gaelic, but the Irish government makes sure that the language is kept alive: For instance, the police force of Ireland is known as Gardaí, meaning Guardians, and the Prime Minister, who we mentioned before, is officially called Taoiseach, which is pronounced something like tea shock. Nobody really knows why they say "President" in English but "Prime Minister" in Irish, not even the Irish themselves; however, those are their official titles. All the street signs are also written in both English and Gaelic.

CHAPTER ONE
Enchanting Myths and Fables

Before Christianity came to Ireland, the island was home to the Celts, an ancient people who also lived in Great Britain and in the places that are now France, Spain, and Portugal. The Irish people of today are the descendants of the Celts, and we still refer to some Irish things as Celtic—even in this very book.

The Celts worshiped many gods and goddesses—in fact, there are 400 known gods worshiped by the Irish Celts alone. Bards told stories and sang songs about these gods and the mortals that met them. These old stories continued to be told for hundreds and thousands of years, shaping Irish folklore and culture.

Let's meet some of the most famous Celtic mythical characters.

TUATHA DÉ DANANN

Most of the gods of Ireland belong to a tribe called the Tuatha Dé Danann, meaning *people of Danu*. Danu was a goddess, but historians don't know much about her. We know that the Tuatha Dé Danann were named after her, but that's about it.

The Tuath Dé used to live in Ireland, which they took from the Fomorians, a race of monstrous creatures that came from under the sea or from underground. The Tuath Dé and the Fomorians were at war with each other for many years before the Fomorians were defeated and left.

> When humans first came to Ireland, it was the Tuath Dé's turn to leave. They moved to The Otherworld, the magical world where they were born and from where they watched over the people of Ireland.

Over time, the Irish became Christian and started believing that these old gods had actually been ancient kings, angels, or fairies, which they call *"Aos Sí"*—pronounced: *"eess shee."*

Legend says that The Otherworld, where these gods or fairies live, can be entered through stone circles and fairy mounds, which are actually burial mounds made by prehistoric people.

THE DAGDA

The king of the Tuath Dé was known as the Dagda. He was represented as a large warrior with a huge club and a booming laugh. He was the god of war, wisdom, and magic, as well as life and death.

> In battle, he used a magic club that could instantly kill nine men at a time with one end. The other end of the club could bring those men back to life.

He had a magical cauldron that could feed as many people as necessary. It could also bring dead people back to life.

THE MORRÍGAN

The wife of the Dagda was the Morrígan, the goddess of war and death.

> She was represented as an old woman by a river, washing the clothes of the soldiers doomed to die, or as a raven, picking the bodies of fallen soldiers after a battle.

BRIGID

Brigid was the daughter of the Dagda. She was the goddess of poetry, smithcraft, fertility, and fire and was one of the most beloved Celtic goddesses.

When Ireland became Christian, most of the old gods were turned into fairies in people's imagination and stopped being worshiped, but Brigid was so popular that she was instead turned into a saint so that people could continue to pray to her.

> Saint Brigid was said to have founded the first female convent in Ireland. Some stories also say that she was the midwife that helped Mary give birth to Jesus.

When Irish slaves were taken to the Caribbean by the British, they talked about their saints to the slaves brought there from Africa, who blended the stories about Christian saints with the stories of their own African deities. Saint Brigid was turned into Maman Brigitte, the goddess-saint of life, death, and fire in Haitian Vodou.

CÚCHULAINN

Cúchulainn—pronounced *"koo-kul-in"*—was an Irish warrior, one of the greatest heroes of Celtic mythology.

He was the son of the god Lugh and fought in many battles for the people of Ulster, the northern region of Ireland.

> Some legends say he had seven fingers in each hand, seven toes in each foot, and seven pupils in each eye. He looked weird.

The name he was born with was Sétanta. One day, he went to dinner at the house of a blacksmith named Culann. Culann's dog attacked Sétanta, who killed it in self-defense. To apologize, the hero agreed to guard the blacksmith's home. During this time, he became known as *the hound of Culann*, which in Irish is *Cú Chulainn.*

DID YOU KNOW?

The Irish name for Ireland, Éire, comes from the goddess Ériu of the Tuatha Dé Danann. Nowadays, she's used as the personification of Ireland, just like Uncle Sam or Lady Liberty are personifications of America. The names of this goddess's sisters, Banba and Fódla, are also used as poetic names for Ireland.

LUGH

Lugh was a warrior and craftsman god. He was worshiped not just in Ireland but throughout the Celtic world under different names. When he was young, he traveled to join the Tuatha Dé Danann. When he arrived at the castle where they lived, the guard at the door refused to let him in. Lugh offered his services as a swordsman, a blacksmith, a poet, a bard, a playwright, a historian, a sorcerer, and a healer, but every time, the guard turned him down, saying they already had all of those. Then Lugh said, "Wait! Do you have anyone who can do all those things at once?" The guard admitted that they hadn't, so he let him in.

FIONN MAC CUMHAILL

He had a cool name and a very cool life. When he was young, he became the apprentice of a poet who was looking for the Salmon of Knowledge, a magical fish that could give divine wisdom to anyone who ate it—but only to one person. Finn was able to catch it, and the poet ordered him to cook it for him. While Finn was frying the salmon, he burnt his thumb on the frying oil and put it in his mouth to ease the pain. That was enough to get the powers of the salmon. Finn suddenly became the wisest man in the world, and his boss became very annoyed.

CHAPTER TWO
The Fascinating Facts of Scenic Spots

Beauty is in the eye of the beholder, but there is no doubt in anyone's mind that Ireland is one of the most beautiful places on Earth. Many of her lakes, mountains, and glens are pleasing to the eye but also interesting places to learn about.

There is a lake in the Wicklow Mountains called Lough Tay. The land where the lake is was once owned by the Guinness family, and the lake's dark waters kind of make it look like it's made of beer instead of water, so the locals call it the Guinness Lake.

·····

There is a small island off the southern coast of Ireland called Skellig Michael. If you're a Star Wars fan, you'll recognize it as the place where most of *The Last Jedi*—2017—was filmed—specifically the scenes in Ahch-To, the island planet where Luke Skywalker lived as a hermit. The local flocks of puffins inspired the creation of the Porgs, the cute alien birds you see in the movie.

·····

Shamrocking Fact!

Skellig Michael is not alone in featuring in international movies. Since the island has such beautiful spots and the locals speak English, many Hollywood and British productions chose to film there, including the *Harry Potter* movies, *Saving Private Ryan*—1998—and even *Game of Thrones*.

Star Wars The Force Awakens Scene filmed on Skellig Michael.

The highest mountain in Ireland is called Carrauntoohil, pronounced "car-un-too-ull." It is over 3,407 ft high and can be found in County Kerry. It's a popular spot for mountain walkers and climbers.

. . . . .

If you go to County Wexford, you'll find the Hook Lighthouse. Built in 1172, it is the oldest working lighthouse in the world.

. . . . .

Some areas in County Mayo have been used as farming fields since prehistoric times. Historians consider them the oldest known farming fields in the world. They were used by the Neolithic ancestors of the Irish people to grow their crops and keep their livestock.

If you're a fan of cool-looking castles and wish to visit all the castles in Ireland... you can probably forget about it because there are 30,000 of them. That is quite a lot of castles for such a tiny island. We still highly recommend that you visit some of them though, they're very beautiful.

. . . . .

If you go to Blarney Castle, you'll find the Blarney Stone. It just looks like a big rock, but legend says that anyone who kisses it will be granted great powers of eloquence and flattery, which means speaking well. Thousands of visitors go there every year to kiss the stone.

. . . . .

Many places in Ireland have names in Gaelic, which can be quite long. The longest place name in the country is Muckanaghederdauhaulia. It is an uninhabited townland in County Galway. The name is 22 letters long and translates to *pig farm between 2 expanses of saltwater.*

. . . . .

Shamrocking Fact!
One of Ireland's most famous religious sites is Saint Patrick's Cathedral in Dublin. People have celebrated mass there for around 1,500 years.

Legend says that Saint Patrick once found the Devil living in a mountain cave and banished him. On his way out, the Devil bit a part of the mountain and spat it out. That bit of spat rock became the Rock of Cashel, in County Tipperary, which you can visit: There's a beautiful medieval chapel and cathedral there. What the Devil was doing in a cave in Ireland, nobody really knows.

Rock of Cashel, in County Tipperary

· · · · ·

If you've heard of the Northern Lights, you probably know that they can be seen in the Nordic countries, Russia, and Canada. Thousands of people visit those places just to see these beautiful colors in the night sky. What most people don't know is that you can also see them in the northern part of Ireland, if you're lucky.

If you go to County Meath, you can visit Newgrange, a prehistoric monument. It looks like a big dome covered in grass, surrounded by stone walls. It served as a burial mound for the people of the Neolithic. It is much older than the pyramids of Giza and slightly older than Stonehenge—slightly here means about 200 years.

The famous County Meath in Ireland

CHAPTER THREE
Delicious Delights and Irish Treats

Food plays an important part in every country's culture, and Irish food is as delightful as Ireland's people.

POTATO

Potatoes are famous for having been loved in Ireland since the 1500s. The Irish had a myriad of ways to cook them, from mashed and boiled to bread—yes, potato bread. While Irish cuisine is very diverse and varied, many dishes are served with a side of potatoes.

DID YOU KNOW?

The most popular Irish brand of potato chips—called "crisps" in Ireland—is Tayto Crisps, which was founded by Joseph Spud Murphy in 1954 and has a mascot called Mr. Tayto: a potato wearing a hat and a nice suit. Murphy named the company Tayto after the way his kids pronounced the word potato.

Tayto Crisps was the first brand to make chips seasoned with different flavors. Before that, chips just tasted like salt. Joe Murphy invented the process of putting flavors into chips, which he used to make the brand's first special flavor: Cheese and Onion. It became so popular that other chip companies all over the world tried to buy the rights to this technique or invent their own process. It is because of Joe that nowadays, every brand of chip comes in different flavors.

Shamrocking Fact!

Tayto Crisps is so popular that they even have their own theme park in County Meath called Tayto Park.

· · · · ·

One of the darkest eras of Irish history is the Potato Famine: In the 1840s, there was the Potato Blight, a plague that ruined potato crops all across Europe, hitting Ireland especially hard. Irish farming consisted mostly of potatoes, which means that suddenly, people had nothing to eat, and the British government—which ruled over Ireland at the time—did very little to help.

· · · · ·

This resulted in over one million people starving to death and many more leaving Ireland for places where they had a chance of a better life, such as Great Britain, the United States, Canada, and Australia. Many of today's Irish-Americans are descended from people who came to the country during this time.

· · · · ·

This grim period in their history changed the Irish forever but in a good way: Ireland is now very active in donating resources and helping other starving nations, as they don't want anyone else to suffer what their ancestors suffered.

․․․․․

One example of this generosity came in 2020 when Ireland raised almost $2 million to help the Navajo and Hopi peoples, who at the time were the communities most affected by the COVID-19 Pandemic in America. This was partially to repay the First Nations people for their own generosity, as the Choctaw donated $170—a lot back then—to Ireland during the Potato Famine.

․․․․․

The Famine also left an impact on Irish cuisine. Since the Blight ended, potatoes are now more loved than ever in the Emerald Isle. They are also traditionally cooked with the skin because the skin also has precious nutrients, and the Irish learned not to let any part of a potato go to waste during the Famine.

DRINKS

The Irish, and their ancestors, have been brewing beer for 5,000 years.

· · · · ·

The Irish are known throughout the world for loving a pint of Guinness, but in reality, this brand of beer is only popular in the Greater Dublin Area, where it is made. The rest of the country prefers other brands, such as Beamish and Murphy's. However, Guinness is the most famous Irish beer worldwide.

· · · · ·

DID YOU KNOW?

The Guinness Brewery, also known as St. James' Gate Brewery, was built on a piece of land bought by the Guinness company in 1759. They signed a contract that allowed Guinness to own that land for 9,000 years. They are that confident that 9,000 years from now, people will still want a pint of Guinness.

· · · · ·

When the Irish drink, it is usually in pubs. Dublin, the capital and the largest city in Ireland, has a staggering 722 pubs.

This probably won't surprise you, but studies have shown that Ireland is one of the biggest beer-drinking countries in the world. The country consumes around 100 L—which is around 26 gal—per person per year.

· · · · ·

The drink that the Irish love even more than beer is whiskey! Fun fact, whiskey made in Ireland is spelled with an "e", but the one made in Scotland is spelled whisky. They spell it differently because both countries are master whiskey–whisky makers, but they have different ways of making it that go back hundreds of years.

· · · · ·

Shamrocking Fact!

American whiskey is also spelled with an E" because American brands use the Irish way of making whiskey, whereas Canadian brands usually make whisky using the Scottish method.

MISCELLANEOUS FOOD

Besides potatoes, the biggest staple in Irish cuisine is probably pork. In fact, historians believe that pigs were the first animals to be domesticated in Ireland, way back in Neolithic times. It is eaten as sausages, bacon, ham, steaks, and gammon.

· · · · ·

Shamrocking Fact!

Northern Ireland catches around 700 t of eels every year, which they then export to the rest of the world.

· · · · ·

Ireland is the biggest importer of bananas in all of Europe. The Irish company Fyffes imports bananas from all over South America and then sells them to the rest of Europe.

· · · · ·

Like the British, the Irish enjoy a good black pudding, which is not a dessert but rather a sausage made of blood taken from a pig or a cow.

· · · · ·

There are around 50 different types of Irish cheese, which are also eaten worldwide.

CHAPTER FOUR
Victorious Sports and Champion Athletes

Ireland has had its fair share of amazing athletes. The Celtic boldness has won quite a few medals.

The most popular sports in Ireland are rugby, soccer—which is called "football" there—Gaelic football, and hurling. Rugby and football were imported from Britain, whereas Gaelic football and hurling are native Irish sports.

. . . . .

Gaelic football is a mix between soccer, American football, and rugby, with a little basketball thrown in since you can dribble the ball as well as kick it and throw it.

Shamrocking Fact!

Hurling is similar to Gaelic football, but the players use a stick called a "hurley." Weirdly, the sport is only called "hurling" when it's played by men. When the players are women, it is called "camogie."

IRELAND IN THE OLYMPICS

The first Irish person to win an Olympic gold medal was John Boland, from Dublin. He competed for the Great Britain and Ireland team, since Ireland was still a part of the British Empire at the time. He won two gold medals in the tennis competition in the very first Modern Olympic Games in Athens in 1896.

·····

Pat O'Callaghan was the first Olympic athlete to win a medal while competing under the Irish flag rather than the British one. He won the gold medal for the hammer throw in the 1928 Summer Olympics, marking the first time the Irish national anthem was played in the Olympics. He later won another gold medal, also for the hammer throw, in the 1932 Olympics.

·····

However, the first athlete to represent Ireland in the Olympics, albeit unofficially, was Tom Kiely, who competed in the 1904 Olympics. Both Britain and the US offered to sponsor him and pay for his expenses, but he chose to represent only Ireland and paid for everything himself. Ireland was not independent at that time, so the Olympic Committee had to include him under the British flag, but he made it very clear that he was there for Ireland.

Kiely competed in that year's all-around competition, which involved 10 different events all on the same day, including a 100-yd run, a mile run, a high jump, a long jump, and a hammer throw. Kiely won the gold medal in that event, thus becoming the first multi-event track and field Olympic champion.

. . . . .

Boxer Francis Barrett was once the youngest Olympian athlete to ever compete for Ireland when he competed in the 1996 Olympics at the age of 19. His record was broken 4 years later by sprinter Martina McCarthy, who competed in the Sydney Olympics when she was 18 years old.

. . . . .

Shamrocking Fact!
The oldest Irish athlete to compete in the Olympics was Denis Carey, who was almost 40 years old when he competed in the 1912 Olympics in the hammer throw competition.

. . . . .

Katie Taylor was the first female Irish boxer to compete in the Olympics. She won a gold medal in the 2012 London Olympics, and that was after having won gold medals in the Women's World Championships and the European Union Championships.

CHAPTER FIVE
Amazing Creatures and Wild Animals

Let's face it, animals are fascinating no matter what country they are from. Here are some fun facts about the animals of Ireland.

Ireland has more sheep than people. It may seem weird, but it's actually not that uncommon: New Zealand, Australia, Syria, Bolivia, and Uruguay also all have a bigger population of sheep than humans.

. . . . .

Ireland may not have snakes, but its wilderness is full of other animals, such as badgers, red foxes, hedgehogs, and deer.

DID YOU KNOW?

Ireland is famous for not having any snakes. It's one of the few places on Earth where you can't find any snakes, and, in fact, the only reptile species that can be found there is the common lizard, which is native to all of Europe and Asia. You can also find sea turtles swimming close to the Irish shores.

• • • • •

Legend says that Ireland has no snakes because Saint Patrick banished them from the island for being evil creatures. In reality, snakes are not eviler than any other animal—some can be dangerous though, so stay clear of them. Also, Saint Patrick didn't need to banish them because there never were any snakes there. There are three species native to the neighboring Great Britain, but none made it to the Emerald Isle.

• • • • •

You can also find gray squirrels, brown rats, and European rabbits in Ireland, but they're not native. People brought them there from England and other parts of Europe.

The Irish hare is larger than most rabbit and hare species. It has long legs but strangely short ears.

. . . . .

The pygmy shrew is the smallest mammal in Ireland. The largest is the red deer, which is sometimes considered Ireland's national animal.

. . . . .

Ireland was once home to the Irish elk, also called the giant deer, an extinct species of deer with huge antlers. Their skeletons have been found in Irish bogs and can now be seen in several museums throughout the country.

. . . . .

Many other large animals used to live in Ireland, especially during the Ice Age, but are now extinct, including the wooly mammoth and the Irish brown bear, which was closely related to modern polar bears and Alaskan brown bears.

The golden eagle went extinct in Ireland in the early 1900s but was reintroduced in 2001 and is now thriving. The white-tailed eagle was reintroduced in 2007 after being extinct there for 200 years. The success of these species encouraged plans to reintroduce many other bird species to Ireland.

· · · · ·

There are an estimated 11,500 species of insect in Ireland, although the real number is probably much higher.

· · · · ·

It may seem weird, but the most dangerous animal in Ireland is... the cow. There are a lot of cattle farms, and cows are large animals that are usually docile but can sometimes become aggressive. Because there are no large predators in Ireland, such as wolves, big cats, or crocodiles, the highest number of human deaths caused by animals was actually caused by cows, making them the most dangerous animal in the country.

· · · · ·

There also used to be gray wolves in Ireland, but they went extinct due to overhunting. We even know when the last Irish gray wolf died: It was killed in 1786, in County Carlow, by a man named John Watson.

The second most dangerous animal in Ireland, oddly enough, does not live in Ireland, but around it: The Portuguese man o' war is a jellyfish-like creature that can be found in the waters around many countries, including Ireland. Their venom is extremely dangerous to most creatures, including humans. Even dead Portuguese man o' wars found on the beach should be left alone.

· · · · ·

In Ireland, the wren—a little European bird—is known as *dreoilín*, meaning trickster. There is an Irish story about the time when the birds were trying to choose their king, so they held a competition to see which one could fly the farthest. The wren knew it was going to lose because it had tiny wings, so it hid in the eagle's feathers. The eagle flew up, farther than any other bird, and just as it reached its limit, the wren shot out of its feathers and flew just a little farther up. The eagle protested, saying it was the strongest bird, and the wren replied, "Oh, yeah? Well, I'm the smartest." And so, the wren was chosen as the King of All Birds, which is how it is still known in Irish folklore.

CHAPTER SIX
Epic Adventures and Folktales

We've talked about the ancient myths of the Celts, but modern Ireland is also full of fun legends and folklore.

LEPRECHAUNS

The most famous Irish mythical being is, of course, the leprechaun: A spirit taking the form of a small man wearing green clothes usually found guarding a pot of gold at the end of a rainbow.

·····

In Ireland, leprechauns are known as the shoemakers of the fairy folk. Their name may come from *leath bhrogan*, which is Irish for shoemaker. If you go wandering into the forests of Ireland, you may hear the tapping of their little hammers as they make shoes for the fairies.

·····

The leprechauns have some close relatives called *clurichauns*. Small beings that look a lot like the leprechauns but are known more for haunting wine cellars and drinking a lot.

Because of the efforts of a group of lobbyists from County Louth, leprechauns are now considered a protected species under European Union law—the same law that protects endangered animals and plants all across Europe. The lobbyists explained that the leprechaun population is shrinking, with only 236 leprechauns living near the town of Carlingford.

· · · · ·

If you're looking for a good movie about leprechauns to watch on Saint Patrick's Day, we recommend Disney's *Darby O'Gill and the Little People*—1959. It is a great representation of Irish culture and folklore, although many of the actors were not actually Irish—including Sean Connery, who was Scottish. We do *not* recommend the *Leprechaun* movies, which are horror films and very much not for kids—and also have very few Irish people in them.

· · · · ·

Shamrocking Fact!

We think of leprechauns as always wearing green, but in early tales, they actually wore red, which was considered the magic color. It was the Irish poet William Allingham that first wrote about leprechauns wearing green.

OTHER CELTIC CRITTERS

There are many other mythical beings in Irish folklore besides leprechauns: The second most famous is probably the banshee, a ghost-like fairy woman who gives out spine-chilling screams. When you hear the banshee's wail, it is a warning that someone is about to die.

· · · · ·

The púca or pooka is another Irish creature: They're shapeshifters who can appear as a black wild dog, a black horse, a human with strange animal-like features, or just as a weird-looking goblin. They like to trick and make fun of humans, but they can also be helpful and warn them of danger. Traditionally, all blackberries left unpicked after Halloween belong to the pooka, so the Irish avoid picking them.

· · · · ·

> Irish port towns have their fair share of stories about mermaids, which are also called merrows there. Nowadays, mermaids are portrayed as beautiful women with fish-tails, but traditionally, Irish merrows were dangerous fish creatures with sharp teeth and pig-like noises that attacked unlucky sailors.

CHAPTER SEVEN
Celebrated Celebrities and Famous Folks

Born on the shores of Éire, but known throughout the world. Here are some fun facts about some famous folk.

Arthur Wellesley (1769-1852), also known as the Duke of Wellington, was the archenemy of Napoleon Bonaparte and served as Prime Minister of the United Kingdom for two terms, despite being born in Dublin, Ireland. This made him both Irish and British, since Ireland was a part of the British Empire at the time. Queen Victoria once said that he was the greatest man ever born in the United Kingdom.

Arthur Wellesley

The submarine was invented by Irish engineer John Philip Holland (1841-1914), who designed it for the U.S. Navy.

·····

Northern Irish actor Liam Neeson, who you may know from the *Taken* films or as Qui-Gon Jinn from *Star Wars*, was a successful boxer when he was a teenager. He also worked as a forklift driver before becoming an actor.

·····

Actress Saoirse Ronan does not like social media but did join Twitter for a short time so she could follow Stephen Fry, a beloved English actor and author.

·····

Irish actors Brendan Gleeson and Domhnall Gleeson, who are father and son, both appeared in the Harry Potter films but played unrelated characters: Brendan played Alastor *Mad-Eye Moody*, and Domhnall played Bill Weasley.

·····

When actor Colin Farrell was young, he was a big fan of Marilyn Monroe. He even left Smarties under his pillow at night for her ghost.

Irish TV show host Graham Norton auditioned for the part of Samwise Gamgee in *The Lord of the Rings*, which ended up being played by Sean Astin. Norton admits that it was probably a good decision, as his audition went pretty badly.

. . . . .

DID YOU KNOW?

Later, when Farrell was 18, he was a suspect in a murder case. While in Sydney, Australia, he was detained by the police because he happened to look exactly like a man suspected of killing a person. Luckily, he was released when one of his friends provided him with an alibi.

CHAPTER EIGHT
Educational Excursions and Literary

Even more than great actors and athletes, Ireland is known for her passionate writers and poets.

OSCAR WILDE

Oscar Wilde is one of the most famous Irish authors of all time, despite only ever having written one novel, *The Picture of Dorian Gray*—1890; although he also wrote children's books and several plays.

· · · · ·

Wilde could speak several languages, including German, French, Italian, and Greek, but couldn't speak Irish.

JAMES JOYCE

Joyce's most famous novel, *Ulysses*—1922—was inspired by Homer's "Odyssey." It takes place in Dublin on June 16, 1904, which was the day when Joyce had his first date with his wife Nora. Joyce's fans still celebrate his works every year on June 16, which has become known as Bloomsday after the novel's protagonist, Leopold Bloom.

· · · · ·

Joyce was a beloved Irish writer, and when he met the equally-beloved American writer Ernest Hemingway, they became drinking buddies. If you walked into a bar in Paris in the 1920s, there was a good chance you would see the two of them getting drunk and picking fights—or rather, Hemingway picked fights while Joyce hid behind him.

· · · · ·

Shamrocking Fact!

Apart from his very confusing novels, James Joyce was also famous for having written very dirty love letters to his wife. One of those letters was sold in an auction in 2004 for over £240,000!

VAMPIRES

Bram Stoker, the author of *Dracula*—1897—was Irish. There's even an annual Bram Stoker festival in Dublin that celebrates this great author. While vampires are creatures from Eastern European folklore and the novel takes place in Transylvania, it is very likely that Stoker also based many of Count Dracula's traits on Ireland's own creepy mythical beings—specifically, on Abhartach, an evil dwarf chieftain who terrorized his people. Every time he was killed, he rose again from his grave, each time more bloodthirsty.

·····

Dracula was one of two novels that basically founded the vampire genre and the way we think of vampires today. The other one was Carmilla—1872—written by Sheridan Le Fanu—who was also Irish! So, if you're a fan of vampires, you have the Irish to thank for.

·····

FUN GOSSIPY FACT:

Stoker was married to Florence Balcombe, who was Oscar Wilde's ex-girlfriend.

OTHER AUTHORS

Jonathan Swift, the author of *Gulliver's Travels*—1726—wrote most of his other books and poems under different names or anonymously. Swift was known for his dry, sarcastic way of writing—so much that the word *Swiftian* is now applied to any work written in the same tone.

· · · · ·

A lot of what we know about Irish folklore comes from the writings of Irish poet William Butler Yeats and playwright Lady Gregory, who compiled stories about leprechauns and fairies from all over the country. They also founded several theaters in Ireland. Yeats won the Nobel Prize in Literature in 1912.

· · · · ·

Nobel Prize-winning Northern Irish author Seamus Heaney loved writing about nature and the countryside... except for one very specific part of nature: He was deadly afraid of frogs.

· · · · ·

Although he spent most of his life in England, teaching at the universities of Oxford and Cambridge, C. S. Lewis, the author of *The Chronicles of Narnia*, was born in Belfast, the capital of Northern Ireland.

CHAPTER NINE
Melodic Memories and Groovy Rhythms

Irish music is one of the most iconic in the world, and many Irish singers and musicians are internationally famous.

DID YOU KNOW?

The harp is used a lot in traditional Irish music. In fact, it has become one of the official symbols of Ireland, used on the back of the Irish Euro coins. Ireland is the only country on Earth to have a musical instrument as its national symbol—that's how important music is to the Irish.

However, you may have noticed that the logo of Guinness is also a harp. They actually chose that as their symbol before the country did, and the Irish government even had to ask permission from the Guinness company to use the harp as the national symbol.

> The oldest harp in Ireland is the Brian Boru harp, made in the year 1014. You can see it on display at Trinity College in Dublin. It was previously held in the Vatican for many years.

· · · · ·

The perfect place to hear some Irish music is at a *céili*—pronounced "kay-lee." It's a traditional Irish gathering full of music and dancing.

· · · · ·

Many people in America call the traditional Irish dance, the one where you keep your upper body stiff and just move your legs a lot, "Riverdance," but it's actually called "step dance." Riverdance is "an Irish performance that uses a lot of step dancing." It was first performed in the 1994 Eurovision Song Contest, and it became so popular that it was turned into a whole musical.

· · · · ·

By the way, the Eurovision Song Contest is a yearly European music and dance competition and is one of the biggest events in Europe. Ireland has won the contest seven times, more times than any other country, and is the only country to have won three times in a row.

The best-selling music acts by Irish performers of all time are U2, The Cranberries, Enya, Van Morrison, and Westlife.

Westlife

· · · · ·

The traditional bagpipes of Ireland are known as uilleann pipes, pronounced: "ill-un." They're different from the Scottish bagpipes—the ones you've probably seen before—because the player doesn't need to blow into the pipes, meaning that an Irish bagpiper can talk and sing while playing.

· · · · ·

One of the most famous Irish songs is "Danny Boy," often sung at funerals, both Irish and American. While its melody comes from a traditional Irish tune, "Londonderry Air," the lyrics were actually written by Frederic Weatherly, who was English.

The banjo is also very popular in Irish music, even though it wasn't invented by the Irish but rather by African slaves in the US.

· · · · ·

The Irish version of scatting is called "lilting": singing nonsense words and syllables that don't make sense, but they sound good.

· · · · ·

Shamrocking Fact!
Another famous Irish folk song is "Dúlamán," which is Irish for channel wrack, a kind of seaweed you can eat.

CHAPTER TEN
Bizarre Bits and Unbelievable Truths

Here are some weird random facts about Ireland and her people.

There are seven times more Americans of Irish descent than there are people in Ireland.

One-third of the Australian population is also of Irish descent. That's 8.5 million people!

Ireland is called the Emerald Isle because of its green pastures and its luscious landscape that stays green all year round.

You may have noticed that many Irish surnames start with "Mac-" or "O'-." This is a traditional way to indicate ancestry; the former means *son of*, and the latter means *grandson of*, and both can be used to just mean descendant of. So *MacDonald* means *son of Donald* and *O'Brien* means *grandson of Brien*.

Many Irish surnames also start with "Fitz-." It comes from Latin *filius*, meaning *son*, so "Fitz" also means, you guessed it, *son of*.

Irish people don't actually say "Top o' the mornin' to ye" when they want to say "Good morning." If you meet an Irish person and they say this, they're probably having a laugh.

It is common in Ireland to express agreement by repeating what was said: "Did you go to school?" "I did go." This is because until recently, the Irish language did not have words for *yes* or *no*, so people repeated the statement instead, and this carried on after they started speaking English.

As of 2023, the current Taoiseach—the Prime Minister of Ireland, remember?—is Leo Varadkar, who is an amazing record breaker: He is not only the youngest person to ever be elected Taoiseach, at 38 years old, but he's also the first person of color—he is of Indian descent—and the first openly gay person to serve as Taoiseach.

Green eyes are more common in Ireland and Scotland than anywhere else in the world. Around 86% of people there are green-eyed.

Ireland has the second highest percentage of redheads in the world: They make up 10% of the population. They are only beaten by Scotland, where redheads make up 13% of the population.

The Irish are famous for being redheads, but actually, there are more Irish blonds than redheads, and the vast majority of the population has dark hair.

Some people believe that the fair-skinned, red-haired Irish people are the true natives of Ireland, and the dark-haired people must be descended from folk who came from somewhere else, like Spain. Actually, scientists have discovered that the dark-haired people are the ones whose ancestors have always been on the island, and the blonds and redheads are descended from the Vikings that once came from the far North of Europe to raid the British Isles.

Ireland is home to a booming entertainment industry. If you're looking for comedy shows to watch, we recommend *Father Ted*, *Derry Girls*, and *Moone Boy*. If you're looking for some beautiful animated epic films, we recommend director Tomm Moore's Irish Folklore Trilogy: *The Secret of Kells* (2009), *Song of the Sea* (2014) and *Wolfwalkers* (2020).

CHAPTER ELEVEN
Unbelievable Irish History Trivia

Ireland has a rich history, full of victories, turmoils, and wars—mostly with the British.

Halloween was greatly inspired by the Celtic festival of Samhain, pronounced: "sow-inn." While the modern word *Halloween* comes from the English *All Hallows' Eve*, most of the traditions that we associate with this day come from Samhain, whose name means *Summer's End*.

. . . . .

> Samhain was "a festival held in Ireland and Great Britain that marked the end of the harvest and the Celtic New Year". The Celts believed that the spirits of the ancestors came back to visit the living, but so did evil spirits. Large bonfires were lit to scare them away. Nowadays, Irish people celebrate Halloween in similar ways to the Americans and the British, but Neopagans all over the world still celebrate Samhain in an original way.

DID YOU KNOW?

Dublin, the capital of Ireland, was not founded by the Irish but by the Vikings who came to raid the coasts of the British Isles. The city was founded as a refuge where the Vikings could get some rest and repair their ships after a long day of pillaging.

· · · · ·

Saint Patrick is the most famous Irish saint. You may be surprised to know that he wasn't actually Irish: He was a Roman born in Great Britain who was brought to Ireland as a slave when he was a boy. He escaped and moved to England, where he became a priest. It was only after that that he returned to Ireland to convert the local pagans to Christianity.

· · · · ·

People abroad associate the four-leaf clover with Ireland and Saint Patrick's Day, but the Irish actually use a normal three-leaf clover to represent the holiday. Legend says Saint Patrick used a shamrock with three leaves to explain the Holy Trinity: How the Father, the Son, and the Holy Spirit are three different things, but they're also all aspects of the same God, just like the three leaves of the shamrock are all part of the same plant..

Shamrocking Fact!

Saint Patrick's Day, March 17, is not his birthday, as many people think, but rather the day he died. In the old days, few people bothered to remember their own birthdays, but when a famous or beloved person died, everybody remembered that date.

Crowds awaiting the beginning of the St. Patrick's Day Parade, Dublin city centre, Ireland.

· · · · ·

The official color of Ireland is actually blue, not green. Green clothes are really only worn by leprechauns—who are Irish, yes, but they're fairies, and therefore not proper Irish citizens—and by Americans celebrating St. Patrick's Day. In fact, the Protestants once outlawed the *wearin' o' the green* in Ireland because it is considered a Catholic color.

Today, the flag of Ireland is green—representing the Catholic population—and orange—representing the Protestant population—with white in the middle to represent the peace between the two communities.

· · · · ·

Ireland was neutral during World War II. The country stayed out of the fight, although many Irishmen volunteered to fight in the British and American armies.

World war II Russian Soviet Red Army soldiers marching through forest.

Also, Ireland would sometimes secretly help the Allies: When a military plane crashed on the island, the Irish would rescue the pilots and treat their injuries no matter which side they belonged to. However, pilots that fought for the Axis powers—Germany and Italy—were detained until the end of the war, but Allied pilots—Americans, British, and French—were taken to the border with Northern Ireland so they could go back to their headquarters.

·····

Even though Ireland was not involved in the war, a German plane bombed Dublin in 1941, causing 34 deaths. To this day, nobody knows why the Germans did it, but there are some theories: Maybe they found out that the Irish were secretly helping the Allies, and this was them warning the Irish to stop and not join the war. Maybe the planes just got turned around, which did happen sometimes.

CHAPTER TWELVE
Tongue Twisters and Celtic Chuckles

We interrupt these fun facts to bring you some different fun stuff.

IRISH TONGUE TWISTERS

You thought tongue twisters were hard in English? Wait until you see these Irish ones!

> *Ná bac le mac an bhacaigh is ní bhacfaidh mac an bhacaigh leat.*
>
> **Translation:** Don't bother the beggarman's son, and the beggarman's son won't bother you.

> *Seacht sicín ina seasamh sa sneachta lá seaca.*
>
> **Translation:** Seven chickens standing in the snow on a frosty day.

> *Fear feargach ag faire na farraige fuaire.*
>
> **Translation:** An angry man watching the cold sea.

IRISH RIDDLES

Here are some traditional Irish riddles for you to work your brain. You can find the answers in the Conclusion of this book. No peeking.

RIDDLE NUMBER 1

Which Irish surname can be spelled with only two letters?

_____

RIDDLE NUMBER 2

How many gold coins can you fit in an empty pot?

_____

RIDDLE NUMBER 3

What can hold water even though it is full of holes?

_____

RIDDLE NUMBER 4

What has eight legs but can't walk?

_____

IRISH JOKES

Be warned: some of these are pretty corny, and some others use Irish stereotypes that are absolutely not true—but they are pretty funny.

What kind of rock is green and light as a feather?

A shamrock!

. . . . .

Why shouldn't you sit on a four-leaf clover?

Because you shouldn't press your luck!

. . . . .

Where is the most disappointing place to find gold?

In the dictionary!

. . . . .

What do ghosts drink on Saint Patrick's Day?

Spirits! Or booze—get it? Boos?

If Saint Patrick had been born during Christmas, what would we call him?

Saint O'Claus!

What is Irish and sits in your backyard all day?

Paddy O'Furniture.

What do you call an Irishman that is bulletproof?

Rick O'Chet!

What do Irish people get after eating Italian food?

Gaelic breath!

. . . . .

What do you call a very large spider in Ireland?

Paddy Longlegs!

. . . . .

Why is it hard to borrow money from a leprechaun?

Because they're a little short.

. . . . .

How do you make an Irish potato have double nationality?

You turn it into a French fry!

A Garda—an Irish police officer—arrests two men on the street and asks them for their names and address. The first one says, "My name is Paddy McCormick, and I don't live anywhere." The second one says, "My name is Fred O'Brien, and I live in the house next to Paddy's!"

. . . . .

Three men from England, Scotland, and Ireland walk into a bar and order three beers. Before they have a chance to drink, three flies fly overhead and fall into each of their drinks. The Englishman gives his drink back to the waiter and orders another one. The Scot takes the fly from his glass, tosses it away, and drinks his beer. The Irishman reaches into his glass, grabs the fly, and screams at it, "Spit it out right now!"

An Englishman asks an Irishman, "How come when you ask an Irishman a question, they always reply with another question?" The Irishman replies, "Nonsense. Who told ye that?"

. . . . .

A Garda knocks on a woman's door and says, "I'm sorry, Mrs. O'Toole, but your husband had an accident in the brewery. He fell into a vat of beer and drowned." The woman says, "Oh, no! Tell me, officer, was it quick?" The Garda says, "Not really. He had to climb out three times to use the bathroom."

. . . . .

An Irishman meets a man from Texas in a bar, and they start talking. The American says that he owns some land back in Texas. The Irishman asks how big his property is. The American says, "Why, if you get into a car at dawn and start driving across my land, you'll only reach the other end by sunset." The Irishman sighs and says, "Aye, I used to have a busted car like that too."

CHAPTER THIRTEEN
Basic Irish Words

If you visit Ireland, you may need to know some useful words and expressions.

All Irish people speak English, but they speak their own dialect of English, which uses expressions that are not used anywhere else. Some of those expressions come from the Irish language, which only a small part of the population can speak. In fact, more people speak Polish than Irish in Ireland. But even the people who don't speak the language still use a few Irish words mixed in with English—just like you can use the word *croissant* even if you don't speak French.

The Irish language is actually one of the oldest living languages in the world, about as old as Hebrew, Chinese, and Ancient Greek.

Here is some lingo that you may come across in Ireland.

COMMON IRISH WORDS AND PHRASES

These are some of the Gaelic words that Irish people often say even when speaking English. First is the word and how it is spelled, then how it is pronounced, then the translation.

Céad mile fáilte. "Ked mee-la fawl-sha."

One hundred thousand welcomes. A common greeting.

Cén t-am é? "Cayn tom ay."

What time is it?

Craic. "Crack."

Fun, good times, as in, "Last night was craic!"

Craic. "Crack."

Fun, good times, as in, "Last night was *craic!*"

Cúla búla. "Coo-luh boo-luh."

Cool.

Cupán Tae. "Cup-awn-tey."

Cup of tea. Used more at home, not really in coffee shops or restaurants.

Dia duit. "Dee-uh dit."

Hello.

Éire. "Eh-ruh."

Ireland.

Go raibh maith agat. "Guh ruh mah a-gut."

Thank you.

Le do thoil. "Led-uh-holl."

Please.

Madra. "Maw-dra."

Dog.

Scéal. "Shkayl."

Story. Used especially in the sentence, "What's the scéal?", meaning "What's new?"

Sláinte. "Slawn-che."

It's what you say when you make a toast, like, "Cheers!" Literally, it means "Health."

Slán. "Slawn."

Literally, it means "Safety," but it is used to say goodbye.

Slán leat. "Slawn lat."

Safety with you. Another way to say goodbye.

Tá brón orm. "Taw bron ur-um."

I'm sorry.

COMMON IRISH ENGLISH EXPRESSIONS

These are some of the expressions you may hear in Ireland. They're not Gaelic, but they're very distinctly Irish.

"Acting the maggot": Being silly.

"Awful good": Very good.

"Bag o' tayto": A bag of potato chips, even if they're not the Tayto brand.

"Cop on": Wise up.

"The craic was 90": That fun we had was really great.

"Doing the messages": Shopping for groceries.

"Donkey's years": Many years.

"Fair play to ye": Well done.

"Flat out": Busy.

"Go way outta that": No way, I don't believe you.

"Grand": Fine, good.

"Great drying out": Nice weather—nice enough that you can put your clothes out to dry.

"How's the form?": How are you doing?

"The Jacks": The bathroom.

"Knackered": Exhausted.

"Lose one's rag": Lose one's temper.

"Not a loss on me": I'm doing well.

"Oul fella": Dad.

"Oul wan": Mom.

"Rashers": Thin bacon slices.

"What's the craic?": What's new? Yes, craic usually means fun, but in this phrase, it means news.

CONCLUSION

That's it, lads and lasses. Those were all the fun facts we had for you. We're done!

… Oh, I guess you'll be wanting the answers to the riddles. Here they are:

1. Casey (KC)
2. None: If you put just one coin in it, it's not an empty pot anymore
3. A sponge
4. Four pairs of trousers

We hope that this book made you appreciate and be interested in the awesome place that is Ireland. It is so much more than leprechauns, St. Patrick's Day, and cultural stereotypes. We hope that from now on, you think of the Emerald Isle every time you hear the gentle notes of a harp, every time you see a raven flying overhead, and definitely every time you eat a potato.

Have some Tayto Crisps on us when you get there. *Slán leat!*

REFERENCES

Ahch-To. (n.d.). Wookieepedia. Retrieved February 10, 2023, from https://starwars.fandom.com/wiki/Ahch-To

Allred, B. (2022, March 25). *Are There Snakes in Ireland?* AZ Animals. https://a-z-animals.com/blog/are-there-snakes-in-ireland/

Amber. (2018, March 17). *Interesting Facts About 9 Great Irish Authors*. Foghorn Review. https://foghornreview.com/fun-facts-9-great-irish-authors/

Celtic Mythology. (n.d.). TV Tropes. Retrieved February 10, 2023, from https://tvtropes.org/pmwiki/pmwiki.php/Myth/CelticMythology

Crabill, E. (2019, July 5*). What You Probably Didn't Know About Irish Sports*. The Odyssey Online. https://www.theodysseyonline.com/irish-sports

Duignan, V. (n.d.). *Old Irish Riddles*. Dúchas.ie. Retrieved February 12, 2023, from https://www.duchas.ie/en/cbes/5009163/4993129/5103018?ChapterID=5009163

Fauna of Ireland Facts for Kids. (n.d.). Kiddle. Retrieved February 14, 2023, from https://kids.kiddle.co/Fauna_of_Ireland

5 Amazing Facts You Never Knew About Irish Food! (n.d.). Irish Taste Club. https://irishtasteclub.com/5-amazing-facts-you-never-knew-about-irish-food/

How Many of These 10 Classic Irish Riddles Can You Solve. (2022, August 29). ? The Irish Post. https://www.irishpost.com/entertainment/10-classic-irish-riddles-brain-teasing-149072

Hutchinson, S. (2018, June 15). *12 Facts About James Joyce*. Mental Floss. https://www.mentalfloss.com/article/547359/facts-about-james-joyce

Ireland. (n.d.). TV Tropes. Retrieved February 8, 2023, from https://tvtropes.org/pmwiki/pmwiki.php/UsefulNotes/Ireland

Irish Potato Famine. (n.d.). TV Tropes. Retrieved February 9, 2023, from https://tvtropes.org/pmwiki/pmwiki.php/UsefulNotes/IrishPotatoFamine

IrishCentral Staff. (2020, June 22). *Leprechauns Are Protected Under European Law*. IrishCentral. https://www.irishcentral.com/roots/leprechauns-protected-european-law

IrishCentral Staff. (2022, May 13). *Some Fun Facts About Leprechauns, Ireland's Most Famous Legend.* IrishCentral. https://www.irishcentral.com/culture/craic/leprechauns-facts

Macdonald, F. (2014, October 21). *Startling Facts About Ireland's Most Famous Writers.* BBC. https://www.bbc.com/culture/article/20140317-james-joyce-in-a-bar-brawl

The Man Who Invented Potato Chip Flavors. (2012, April 20). HuffPost. https://www.huffpost.com/entry/joe-spud-murphy-the-man-w_n_1437270

Momma, W. (2022, February 17). *Irish Words and Phrases We Still Use Every Day* [Video]. YouTube. https://www.youtube.com/watch?v=P97CgCF_4ck

Natasha. (2023, January 1). *30 Fun Facts About Ireland You Should Know.* The World Pursuit. https://theworldpursuit.com/facts-about-ireland/

National Geographic. (2008). *Essential Visual History of World Mythology.* National Geographic Society.

O'Hara, K. (2022, December 19). *31 of the Best Irish Jokes* (That Are Actually Funny). The Irish Road Trip. https://www.theirishroadtrip.com/funny-irish-jokes/

O'Sullivan, L. (2022, March 29). *26 Common Irish Sayings and Meanings.* The Irish Store. https://www.theirishstore.com/blog/26-common-irish-sayings/

Oireland. (n.d.). TV Tropes. Retrieved February 8, 2023, from https://tvtropes.org/pmwiki/pmwiki.php/Main/Oireland

Pat O'Callaghan. (n.d.). Wikipedia. Retrieved February 11, 2023, from https://en.wikipedia.org/wiki/Pat_O%27Callaghan

10 Fun Facts About Ireland. (2021, August 12). Hillwalk Tours. https://www.hillwalktours.com/walking-hiking-blog/10-fun-facts-about-ireland/

The Planet D. (2021a, March 15). *Facts About St. Patrick's Day to Help you Celebrate at Home.* The Planet D. https://theplanetd.com/facts-about-st-patricks-day/

The Planet D. (2021b, July 16). *16 Fun Facts About Ireland You Didn't Already Know.* The Planet D. https://theplanetd.com/facts-about-ireland/

Poleon, J. (2020, September 15). *Top 10 Crazy Facts About Irish Food You Never Knew.* Meanwhile in Ireland. https://meanwhileinireland.com/top-10-mad-facts-about-irish-food-you-never-knew/

Quinn, E. (2020, January 2). *Irish Language Guide.* Wilderness Ireland. https://www.wildernessireland.com/blog/irish-language-guide/

Rana, A. (2020). *How the Wren Became the King of All Birds.* RTE.IE. https://www.rte.ie/brainstorm/2020/1218/1185007-wren-st-stephens-day-ireland-folklore-traditions-bad-luck/

17 Fascinating Facts About Irish Music. (2013, March 6). Soundscaping Source. https://soundscapingsource.com/17-fascinating-facts-about-irish-music/

Shamasunder, S., & Krishtel, P. (2021, May 10). *Opinion: What Native Americans Can Teach Rich Nations About Generosity in a Pandemic.* NPR. https://www.npr.org/sections/goatsandsoda/2021/05/10/994254810/opinion-what-native-americans-can-teach-us-about-generosity-in-a-pandemic

Sheehan, M. (2016, December 12). *15 Things You May Not Know About Oscar Wilde.* Culture Trip. https://theculturetrip.com/europe/ireland/articles/15-things-you-may-not-know-about-oscar-wilde/

Sloan, L. (2019, October 10). *10 Amazing Animal Species Native to Ireland.* Ireland Before You Die. https://www.irelandbeforeyoudie.com/10-amazing-animal-species-native-to-ireland/

10 Fun Facts About Irish Food You Never Knew. (n.d.). Five Roses Pub. Retrieved February 10, 2023, from https://www.fiverosespub.com/news-item/10-fun-facts-about-irish-food-you-never-knew/

Tongue Twisters in Irish. (n.d.). Omniglot. Retrieved February 12, 2023, from https://omniglot.com/language/tonguetwisters/irish.htm

Wallace, N. (2020, May 13). *The 10 Most Famous Irish Myths and Legends of All-Time.* Ireland before You Die. https://www.irelandbeforeyoudie.com/the-10-most-famous-myths-and-legends-from-irish-folklore/

Walsh, J. (2012, July 28). *Top Ten Interesting Facts About Irish Olympic History.* IrishCentral. https://www.irishcentral.com/sports/top-ten-interesting-facts-about-irish-olympic-history-164125256-237518051

Wilson, J. (2022, September 2). *7 Most Dangerous Animals in Ireland (Some Are Deadly).* Animal Vivid. https://animalvivid.com/dangerous-animals-in-ireland/

THANK YOU!

We hope this book made you want to visit Ireland. It is a beautiful, ancient place, full of friendly people and amazing sights. The culture, the music, and the stories are all fascinating and complex; we didn't half do them justice here. There is a whole lot more to see.

If you've enjoyed this book, please leave a positive review on Amazon. We'd really appreciate it!

Made in the USA
Middletown, DE
24 May 2023